Original title:
Wildwood Whispers

Copyright © 2025 Creative Arts Management OÜ
All rights reserved.

Author: Liam Sterling
ISBN HARDBACK: 978-1-80566-700-1
ISBN PAPERBACK: 978-1-80566-985-2

Canvas of Autumn's Palette

Leaves dance down in a bright parade,
Squirrels stash acorns, they're well laid.
Pumpkin spice lattes, oh what a treat,
Forget the gym, my couch is my seat.

Bright oranges, reds—it's nature's best art,
Birds giggle as rustling leaves do depart.
A raccoon in a hat, what a sight to behold,
In this colorful forest, no fun to withhold.

Hidden Paths of the Curious Doe

In the thick brush, a doe peeks through,
Wearing sunglasses, think she's too cool for you.
She prances past mushrooms, all polka-dotted,
Bouncing with joy, her dance is well spotted.

'The grass is greener,' she winks with flair,
Enjoys the gossip of the raccoons' affair.
As she tiptoes home, her secrets she'll keep,
Belly laughs echo as shadows go deep.

Yearning of the Skylark's Flight

A skylark buzzes, she's got rhythm and rhyme,
With a sense of style, she's totally sublime.
She dips and she dives, a feathered ballet,
While onlookers chuckle, "Is she lost or on play?"

Her tunes are contagious, a giggle in the breeze,
Dancing in circles, around all the trees.
For every note sung, a chipmunk will cheer,
Her flight a circus, oh how she draws near.

Revelry in the Misty Dawn

Misty mornings bring creatures alive,
Frogs in top hats start to jive.
Bunnies tap dance, with carrots they sway,
A wild woodland party at the break of day.

'Who invited the owls?' a squirrel will quiz,
'Not me, but I love their hooting fizz!'
With laughter and prancing, the sun starts to rise,
Under arched branches, the fun never dies.

Dialogue of the Wooded Realm

In the trees, the squirrels plan,
Stealing snacks from every man.
They chatter and they run about,
Plotting how to sneak a sprout.

A raccoon with a fancy hat,
Thinks he's quite the noble chap.
But when he trips, what a display,
He swears he meant to dance that way.

The owl hoots with a knowing grin,
As the rabbit pulls a silly spin.
They play a game of tag in flight,
While fireflies blink with all their might.

The brook shares tales of fishy fears,
Of bait and hooks that bring them tears.
It's all a laugh in nature's hold,
As secrets from the forest are told.

Whispers in the Wind's Embrace

The breeze tickles leaves with glee,
A bushy tail peeks out to see.
It quips, 'I've got some jokes to share,
Did you hear the one about the bear?'

A wizard frog croaks by the pond,
With spells for flies—he's quite the bond.
He leaps and lands with a squishy plop,
While giggling toads just can't stop.

A fox in socks holds court at dusk,
With puns that make the mushrooms musk.
They laugh so loud that all are near,
In forest halls, there's nothing to fear.

The wind it swirls with playful ease,
While splats of mud are sure to please.
Each whisper tickles nature's muse,
Where laughter blooms, you can't refuse.

Echoes from the Heart of Nature

The bees buzz news of flower fights,
While petals argue who's the brightest.
One sunflower stands, proud and tall,
And whispers, 'I'm the best of all.'

A hedgehog stumbles, all covered in leaves,
As the story of lunch takes a few leaves.
The forest chuckles from every tree,
As he blushes under a bushy degree.

The deer play charades beneath the moon,
Antlers dancing in a charming tune.
They mimic a stoic rock so well,
That nearby squirrels can hardly quell.

The echoes laugh with every turn,
With secrets of nature's quirky churn.
For every creature has its say,
In this woodland jibber-jabber play.

Moonlit Secrets of the Sylvan Press

Underneath the silver light,
A cricket's got a gig to invite.
He croons his tune with a funny twist,
And every bug just can't resist.

The hedgehogs gather to hear his song,
While fireflies blink and join along.
'What's the buzz?' they giggle and cheer,
A night of plays, it's their time of year.

The fox tells tales of a sneaky hare,
Who thought he could win with a wild flair.
But slipping on dew, oh what a sight,
He joined the dance—what a sweet fright!

As branches sway and shadows prance,
Nature's quirks throw a big, wide glance.
With each moonlit secret shared anew,
In this forest party, there's always a view.

Lullabies of the Wandering Breeze

A breeze snuck in with a giggle,
It tickled the leaves, oh how they wriggle.
The branches laughed, swayed left and right,
Whispering secrets into the night.

Squirrels danced in a twirl and leap,
While owls hooted their nightly 'eep'.
The moon shone bright just to tease,
Plucking stars from the night's cool breeze.

Frogs croaked in a chorus, quite loud,
Joking around, feeling so proud.
The shadows curled, played peek and boo,
In this garden of laughter under the blue.

Enchanted Echoes of the Woodlands

In a glen where laughter nests,
Animals wearing party vests.
A deer spun round with a playful hop,
While rabbits clapped, 'Oh please, don't stop!'

The brook giggled, bubbles afloat,
As frogs shared jokes, snickering remote.
A hedgehog brought pie, oh what a treat,
They dined on dandelions, quite the feat!

Every rustle held a chuckle or two,
Even the bugs chirped, 'Aye, howdy-do!'
The sun threw sparkles, winking at trees,
As nature's laughter danced in the breeze.

The Language of Rustling Leaves

Leaves are gossiping, can't you tell?
They're sharing tales, some odd, some swell.
Acorns dropped in a fit of delight,
Causing a stir in the soft moonlight.

The wind was a prankster, don't you see?
Kicking up dust, playing hide-and-seek.
A branch waved hello, a twig waved back,
In this whimsical dance, nothing they lack.

Trees shrugged off worries, embraced the fun,
While critters played racing, no need to run.
A chorus erupted quite out of the blue,
With nature's own band, what a wild crew!

Beneath the Boughs of Memory

Under the branches, stories collide,
Where giggles of critters hide with pride.
A past of mischief, under leaves thick,
Willow trees whisper their finest trick.

Yesterday's laughter still roams about,
As mushrooms debate with a very loud shout.
Even the rocks stifled a grin,
In their silent world, fun draws them in.

With shadows that dance, frolicsome sprites,
Chasing their tails till the end of nights.
Here in this realm where giggles arise,
Nature spins tales that never say die.

The Poem of Sunlit Clearings

In sunlit nooks where shadows play,
Squirrels gossip all the day.
With acorn hats and tiny shoes,
They plan their pranks, spread silly news.

The rabbits hop with joyful zest,
Who knew that carrots could be jest?
They race and twirl, then take a bow,
To claim the award for best 'Wow!'

The birds up high in trees so round,
Sing silly songs without a sound.
They giggle soft and bend the air,
While butterflies dance without a care.

So in this place where laughter's bright,
Nature's jesters take their flight.
With every rustle, every cheer,
The forest laughs, let out a cheer!

Chants of the Midnight Thicket

In midnight's veil, the owls convene,
With wise old jokes, they laugh unseen.
The crickets chirp their funny tune,
While fireflies flash like stars at noon.

A raccoon wears a mask of fame,
And swipes the snacks, oh what a game!
With wiggles, wobbles, and a frown,
It trips and rolls without a sound.

The bushes rustle, secrets shared,
A badger slips, it's unprepared.
With tumbling twilight, all delight,
As giggles echo in the night.

So let us dance when shadows sway,
In thicket bright, we laugh and play.
With every sound, the night won't rest,
For fun creates the very best!

Secrets in the Mossy Mists

In morning mists where whispers cling,
The hedgehogs plot and laugh, oh zing!
A tale of snails that won the race,
Though slow and steady, won first place.

The toads align for croaky plans,
To start a band with warty hands.
They dream of fame in swampy sings,
What trouble such a chorus brings?

In dampened grass, the mushrooms giggle,
Reciting puns that make you wiggle.
While fog rolls in, they toast with cheer,
To friendships forged, and snacks so near.

Secrets swirl in mists that tease,
While nature chuckles in the breeze.
In every nook, there's fun to find,
As laughter blooms, all will unwind!

The Symphony of Swaying Branches

When branches sway, they start to hum,
A tune that wiggles, what a drum!
The leaves all clap in cheerful glee,
As squirrels join in with a zany spree.

The winds blow soft, what melodies,
As chipmunks dance like it's a breeze.
With little feet that never stop,
They stomp and twirl till branches drop.

A wren sings high, a crow sings low,
Together creating quite the show.
They joke about who flies the best,
While branches sway, it's quite the jest!

In this grand symphony of play,
With every rustle, life's array.
The woodland's whispers, a joyful sound,
In every heart, their fun is found!

The Allure of the Forest's Veil

In a forest where trees play tricks,
Squirrels wear hats and do silly flicks.
The mushrooms all giggle, they wiggle around,
While the bushes throw parties with no one around.

A bear with a bowtie struts through the grove,
He's searching for honey but ends up in a stove.
The rabbits are laughing in raucous delight,
As they turn on the lights for a wild disco night.

The owls twist and twirl in their grand little show,
While deer play charades in the moonlight's soft glow.
The raccoons in tuxedos, quite dapper indeed,
Are auctioning acorns with eccentric speed.

Just follow the giggles, the quirks, and the quirks,
In this whimsical world where the forest just smirks.
With each rustle and chuckle, you'll see it's all true,
The allure of the veil—oh, what fun's waiting for you!

Hidden Murmurs of Solitude

In the hush of the trees, a squirrel starts singing,
While the leaves join in, their chorus just clinging.
A turtle's slow dance, so grand and so bold,
Makes the shadows giggle, or so I'm told.

A raccoon with dreams of chasing the moon,
Turns into a jester, makes everyone swoon.
The frogs in their crowns hold a splendid soirée,
With crickets as DJs, they're jamming away.

High above in the branches, two owls debate,
About who can hoot louder, it's quite the estate.
And under the ferns, all the bugs have a dance,
With moves that could win them a local romance.

So tune into whispers, the giggles, the fun,
In the secrets of solitude, laughter's never done.
With each rustle and giggle that floats through the air,
Hidden murmurs remind us there's joy everywhere!

Hush of the Ancient Roots

Under the trees, secrets grow,
Squirrels plot, and the winds blow.
Old roots chuckle in the deep,
While owls snicker, they rarely sleep.

Fungi dance with a twist and twirl,
Mushrooms giggle, creating a whirl.
The earth jokes with the ants on parade,
As rabbits laugh at the plans they've laid.

Vines tickle branches high and low,
A dance-off starts with a lively show.
Old roots holler, 'We can still groove!'
A woodsy party in every move.

Now hear the crackle of hidden pranks,
Pinecones tumble, the forest wanks.
Nature thrives in playful jest,
In the hush of roots, we find the best.

Harmony Among the Whispering Pines

Among the pines, there's a silly tune,
The breeze giggles, a playful boon.
The branches sway, they know the trick,
Play hide and seek, it's all quite quick.

The owls hoot with a wink and grin,
While squirrels play loose, no fear of sin.
Saplings sway as if they know,
That comedy blooms wherever they grow.

A ruckus erupts with a rustle and shake,
Leaves burst out laughing, what a mistake!
The tree trunks join in with a hearty roar,
Nature's joke echoes, who could ask for more?

As light fades, the shadows dance,
Each creak and crackle gives chance to prance.
In harmony, we find that we pine,
For silly moments, oh, how divine!

Resonance of the Feathered Choir

In branches high, the birds convene,
A feathered choir, a sight unseen.
Chirps and tweets in a cacophony,
Who knew a nest could host a symphony?

Cardinals boast with a blushing note,
While sparrows giggle, 'Aren't we remote?'
Woodpeckers knock, 'Let's start the show,'
The audience rustles, 'Oh, look out below!'

In harmony, they jest and tease,
Fluffy feathers dance with ease.
As night falls, they start their refrain,
'Get your tickets, this is our main!'

Echoes of laughter under the moon,
A chorus of chuckles, a droll cartoon.
Each little bird, a comic star,
In the woods where fun travels far.

Magic in the Mossy Mandolin

A mandolin played by a gnome so spry,
With moss and dew, it reached the sky.
Each pluck was met with a wiggle and jump,
Frogs in tuxedos began to thump.

The forest floor became the stage,
Where critters cheered, they flipped a page.
The breeze would laugh and tease the leaves,
As if the melody conjured eaves.

From under rocks, a rabbit pranced,
His two-step moves left many entranced.
The dancer snickered, "Can you keep up?"
While fireflies formed a sparkling cup.

Magic lingers on notes that soar,
While mushrooms clap to the gnome's encore.
In twilight's glow, their spirits unite,
A whimsy tale of joy and delight.

Flickering Glimmers of Fireflies

In the dark dance, bugs aglow,
They twirl and spin, a cute little show.
With giggles of light, they play their part,
A cheeky waltz, a firefly heart.

They tease the night with flickering calls,
Like tiny stars that play on the walls.
"Catch me if you can!" they flit and dart,
A glowing game, a bug's fine art.

With each tiny flash, they bring a grin,
And in the tall grass, the fun begins.
These silly lights, in a cosmic spree,
Brought laughter to woods, that's plain to see.

As morning creeps, their show must end,
They bow to the sun, our glowing friends.
Now dreams of their dance will surely stay,
'Neath moonlit beams, in the light of day.

The Stitching of Nature's Fabric

Through leafy seams and twiggy seams,
Nature's patchwork bursts with dreams.
A squirrel sews with a nutty thread,
While a wise old owl shakes his head.

A tapestry of colors bright,
Nature's humor in every sight.
With flowers laughing, bees in flight,
The forest grins, a joyous sight.

Beneath the boughs, a rustling sound,
The critters plot, mischief abound.
Twigs and moss—their sewing kit,
Stitches of fun, they never quit.

With every stitch, a tale unfolds,
From playful pranks to secrets bold.
The forest giggles in unison,
A crafted world of joy for fun.

The Voice of the Evergreen

Oh, the tall trees whisper with glee,
Beneath their boughs, all is free.
"Want shade?" they joke, with branches wide,
In their green hearts, laughter does reside.

Their needles chuckle, sway and bend,
Each gust brings tales from branch to end.
With humor hidden in every leaf,
These ancient giants foil all grief.

Squirrels scamper, with a joke or two,
"Don't leaf us now!" they cry anew.
The evergreens hum, in twilight's warm kiss,
Nature's jesters, wrapped in bliss.

When summer comes, oh, how they sway,
With breezy banter, they steal the day.
In this forest so green, full of cheer,
The voice of the trees is crystal clear.

Tales Held by the Gnarled Roots

In tangled roots, stories hide,
Of mischief and fun, where critters bide.
A wise old tortoise spins a yarn,
Of how he danced with a polka-dot barn.

Fungi giggle, sprouting in clusters,
Marshmallow hats on their quirky blusters.
"We're quite a fun guy!" they yell with glee,
Making the forest burst with esprit.

Down in the soil, a secret club,
Where worms plot pranks in a cozy tub.
With whispers of jokes beneath the ground,
Their earthy laughter knows no bound.

Each knot and twist, a tale unspooled,
Of woodland antics where all are fooled.
In roots so gnarled, the fun remains,
Nature's laughter in every vein.

Rhapsody of the Gentle Breeze

Dancing leaves spin with glee,
A squirrel drops acorns with spree.
Rabbits hop, their tails a blur,
While giggling birds tease and stir.

The breeze tickles trees so high,
Whispers secrets as it passes by.
"Hey, watch your step!" the flowers shout,
As a clumsy deer stomps about.

Little mushrooms don their hats,
Mice play cards with crafty bats.
Laughter echoes through the glade,
As the woodland's charm is displayed.

Nature's jesters, full of cheer,
Making every moment dear.
In this silly, vibrant play,
A world where joy leads the way.

Exploration of the Verdant Mirage

Beneath the leaves, a picnic spreads,
Bugs audition for dance instead.
An owl winks from his high throne,
"Who's a wise guy? Now that's been shown!"

Frogs serenade with a croak,
While ants march in, they're no joke.
In the trees, the whispers fly,
\"Hey, can you spot that lizard guy?\"

Each critter holds a curious tale,
Spinning yarns both wild and pale.
Chasing trails of shimmering light,
They gather 'round for stories at night.

Giggles echo through the lush,
As squirrels rustle, and mushrooms blush.
With every stomp, a new delight,
In this mirage, where dreams take flight.

The Timeless Dance of Scattered Leaves

Leaves pirouette down to the ground,
As a funky beat echoes around.
Everyone joins in, a woodland bash,
With a owl DJ spinning a crash!

The beavers dance with lumber grace,
While hedgehogs roll in a prickly race.
Squirrels throw acorns in the air,
Churning up laughter everywhere.

Bunnies tap-dance on tiny toes,
While fireflies put on a light show pose.
Nature swings, the night goes on,
With beats that bounce till the break of dawn.

In this dance, all worries cease,
As every creature moves with peace.
Embracing fun in every way,
Let the rhythm guide the play!

Hushed Conversations of the Woodland Creatures

In a circle, the critters convene,
Sharing secrets that must be seen.
A turtle whispers, slow and wise,
While fireflies blink in bright disguise.

Dancing shadows, an inner jest,
With a raccoon sharing his best quest.
"Ever tried a berry-flavored snack?"
They all gasp as he fills his pack.

The hedgehog chuckles, rolling about,
"I'd join in, but I'm just worn out!"
Laughter spreads like pollen in bloom,
As giggles chase away the gloom.

Each creature's tale, a humor-filled spree,
Creating joy beneath the canopy.
In this hush, a raucous cheer,
As friendships blossom year after year.

Embrace of the Enchanted Glade

In a glade where shadows play,
Bunny dances, led astray.
Squirrel sings with such delight,
While mushrooms glow with dreams at night.

Fairy hats on gnomes too tall,
They trip and stumble, then they fall.
A jig of joy beneath the pine,
With squirrel cheers that feel divine.

The owl hoots jokes, oh so sly,
Echoes crackle through the sky.
Laughter echoes, wild and free,
In a world of whimsy, just like me.

Serenade of the Sylvan Silence

A turtledove sings off-key,
While frogs croak harmonies with glee.
Bees hum tunes, though slightly strayed,
Creating music in the glade.

The trees wear hats made of moss,
As squirrels play a game of toss.
The sunlight dances on the leaves,
While dandelions play tricks and tease.

Raccoons hold a midnight feast,
With cupcakes made for the very least.
They giggle on the picnic spread,
While dreaming up their lives ahead.

Dreams of the Twisting Vines

Vines twist in a silly way,
Hugging trees like they want to play.
Laughter bubbles from the brook,
Where fish plot mischief and take a look.

The rabbits wear their Sunday best,
Hopping 'round to find the fest.
Toadstools groan at all the pranks,
As humans join in, giving thanks.

The stars peek through the leafy green,
Whispering secrets, unseen yet keen.
Glowing fireflies dance like glee,
In a tangle of joy, wild and free.

The Call of the Hidden Thicket

Behind the ferns, a giggle sounds,
As critters share their wacky rounds.
Bears wear shades, so very cool,
While hedgehogs break out of their school.

A grand parade of ants in line,
Marching proudly, feeling fine.
They tip their hats to passing deer,
And whisper jokes that not all hear.

The thicket hums a tune of cheer,
With every rustle, magic's near.
In this land of laughter's balm,
Every moment feels like a calm.

The Touch of Dew on a Still Morning

The grass giggles, wearing a veil,
It's dressed in jewels, you can't curtail.
A spider yawned, stretched its legs to play,
While ants march on, like they own the day.

Dew drops dance, in a wobbly waltz,
Nature's disco, without a fault.
The sun peeks through, a playful tease,
Makes everyone sparkle, including the bees.

A squirrel jogs, in his puffy coat,
Singing to birds, who'll join his note.
He twirls around, on a branch so spry,
While stick bugs join, as they crawl by.

Laughter echoes through every nook,
As the world smiles; come take a look!
With each glistening drop, there's a joke on cue,
A morning chorus, where nature's the crew.

Breaths of the Ancient Earth

Underneath the roots, secrets churn,
In the soil where mischievous critters learn.
Worms hold a conference, debating the best,
While trees chuckle softly, in their leafy jest.

The rocks grumble, but they just can't hide,
Their age-old wisdom is hard to bide.
A beetle rolls by, with a tiny trophy,
Claiming to be the champ of the mopey.

Moss whispers tales of the damp and the spry,
Of fairies that giggle, and clouds up high.
Each breeze brings a story that tickles the mind,
Of ancient dance parties, so brazenly unlined.

Roots tickle roots, and they laugh in the night,
Sharing old stories, till the morning light.
As laughter bubbles up from the earth's deep throat,
Even stones crack a smile, or so I wrote.

The Gentle Art of Soft Shadows

Shadows stretch, doing the cha-cha,
As the sun pulls back, like a magic car.
A bunny hops, it's a twilight race,
While the trees bob along, keeping pace.

The moon winks down, with a giggling sigh,
And stars throw confetti, in the navy sky.
Each shadow croons, in a silly tone,
While crickets play bass, in a rhythmic drone.

Fireflies twinkle, in a game of hide,
While owls hoot softly, full of pride.
A raccoon tries a funky new stance,
Tripping over shadows, in his nightly dance.

Laughter waltzes, between tree and glade,
Every critter joins in, no need for a parade.
With jests that flutter, through the darkened night,
Whispers twine together, what a joyful sight!

Timeless Tales from the Wilderness

A bear with a hat tells tales of the stars,
While dancing with critters, at their wild bars.
The raccoons toast, with acorn-filled cups,
As the owl spins yarns that get everyone pumped.

The fish splash tales, of the great pond wars,
Where frogs held matches, and chirps won scores.
The turtles nod wisely, with a grin on their face,
Saying, "Slow and steady wins every race!"

There's laughter and music, in every dark glen,
With stories of mischief and mischievous men.
Snakes tell of dances, that twist and glide,
While the fireflies giggle, lighting up the ride.

As the moon chuckles soft, from its seat in the sky,
Each tale exchanged makes the night time fly.
In the wilderness echoes, a chorus so bold,
Funny old stories, forever retold.

The Lost Echo of the Pebbled Stream

In the glimmer of the brook, a sound,
A fish whispers, 'Don't dive, I'm not around!'
The pebbles giggle, skipping in delight,
While frogs hold a concert by the soft moonlight.

A snail slides by, sporting a bright tie,
Claiming it's fancy, though no one knows why.
The crickets chirp in a rhythmic mess,
As dragonflies dance in a game of chess.

When raccoons drop in for a late-night feast,
The echo of laughter grows with each beast.
A squirrel joins in, with a nut in his hand,
Saying, "This party's way better than planned!"

So the stream chuckles, full of life and jest,
Each ripple a joke, a bubbly quest.
With every splash, the night rolls on by,
Sharing its secrets, a feathery sigh.

Nostalgia of the Gnarled Branches

Beneath twisted limbs, where the shadows creep,
The owls recount tales while the shadows sleep.
A crow tells a story of shoes lost in mud,
While pinecones giggle, 'That's too much crud!'

The branches wave gently, like they're on a spree,
"Who'll join the tree dance? Come dance with me!"
But ants in a row are way too uptight,
Pointing at each other, "You stepped on my right!"

A woodpecker knocks with a rhythm profound,
Saying, "Hold your peace, I'm the king of this ground!"
Then squirrels go tumbling, all caught in a spin,
Chasing their tails like a circus within.

With each creak and crackle, the trees play a tune,
Singing their secrets beneath the bright moon.
A leaf falls down saying, "I'm just passing through,"
Laughing at life as it dances anew.

Breath of the Awakening Glade

In the glade where the daisies nod, so spry,
A bear dances sideways, making all critters sigh.
"Hurry up, pinecones!" he bellows with glee,
"Let's turn this old forest into a jamboree!"

The grass whispers secrets of butterflies bold,
While rabbits hop in their jackets of gold.
A hedgehog complains about being too slow,
"Why can't we do more than just bask in the glow?"

The sunlight tickles each leaf on a spree,
As chipmunks collaborate in a wild jubilee.
"You bring the acorns, I'll bring the cheer!"
Frogs join the fun, croaking tunes from the rear.

The glade stretches wide, with laughter and sights,
Chasing away shadows, igniting the nights.
In this lively arena, where antics never fade,
Joy echoes loudly in the sun-kissed glade.

The Resounding Rapture of Raindrops

When raindrops land in a puddle, then splash,
Each drop holds a joke, a chuckle, a dash.
"Catch my hat!" says a frog with a grin,
As clouds burst with laughter, let the fun begin!

A squirrel jumps high, dodging drops with flair,
"Rain dance is marvelous, without a care!"
While beetles decide it's a cabaret night,
Twirling in puddles, all silver and bright.

The trees join the chorus, swaying so free,
"Raindrops can tickle, just wait and see!"
And the whole forest giggles, what a grand show,
As droplets keep drumming on roofs down below.

With every new shower, the joy's on display,
In the puddled fun, worries wash away.
In this symphony sung when the heavens may weep,
There's laughter in every droplet, a joy we can keep.

Songs of the Sylvan Dawn

A squirrel recites a silly tune,
While raccoons dance beneath the moon.
The owls hoot a giggling rhyme,
Making the flowers laugh in time.

The fox trots by with a jaunty hat,
Chasing a butterfly, fancy that!
The trees sway gently, the breeze joins in,
Creating a chorus, where fun begins.

A hedgehog juggles acorns with glee,
As minnows splash in a game of spree.
The brook bubbles up with a cheeky splash,
While frogs croak jokes, making quite the bash.

In this lively glade, the laughter spreads,
As teddies sip tea on little beds.
Nature sings its merry refrain,
In the heart of the woods, joy shall remain.

Whispers of the Verdant Haven

A rabbit races in a carrot suit,
With dancing ants, it's quite a hoot!
The daisies are gossiping, oh so quick,
Hiding secrets that make you tick.

Sunbeams tickle the years of trees,
As chipmunks play catch with the buzzing bees.
A badger snores under a mushroom dome,
Snoring rhymes that echo the loam.

The butterflies wear coats of bright hue,
They flutter and giggle, oh what a view!
The wind tells tales, silly and free,
Of the antics of all, including me!

In this haven of laughter, the days drift by,
As everyone joins the jolly sky high.
Nature's whimsy lights up the day,
In this verdant glen where we laugh and play.

Shadows and Light in the Thicket

A shadow cat crawls with a sneaky grin,
While fireflies dance, lighting up the din.
The sun peeks out, like it's playing hide,
Amidst the bushes, there's nowhere to bide.

The zany deer wear bow ties and vests,
Judging the best of the woodland quests.
Squirrels pull pranks, such a crafty bunch,
As woodpeckers play drums for a forest lunch.

The light falls softly on the silly strife,
As crickets debate the meaning of life.
A wise old owl chuckles in time,
As nature hums its own little rhyme.

In shadows and light, laughter ignites,
Buzzing and chirping through long, starry nights.
The thicket's a stage for the quirkiest play,
Where every creature joins in the fray.

The Forest's Silent Dialogue

The trees shuffle gossip in rustling leaves,
While mushrooms chuckle at what one believes.
A beetle in braces struts down the lane,
Making all wonder if it's all in vain.

The gnomes share jokes with the lurking trolls,
While geese on a pond argue their roles.
A fox plays chess with a clever hare,
Wondering if the game is truly fair.

Sunshine winks as it peeks through the boughs,
As the forest chuckles and takes a bow.
With every rustle and joyous shout,
Nature's dialogue is what it's about.

In this camaraderie of leafy delight,
The forest breathes laughter deep into the night.
With each funny moment, we dance and sway,
In this woodland magic, we find our way.

Whims of the Wandering Breeze

A squirrel in a jaunty hat,
Is chasing clouds, what fun is that!
He hops and twirls, quite out of place,
While dances leave us in a race.

A feather floats, the duck does quack,
It's spinning 'round on nature's track.
With giggles bright and silly snorts,
The trees sway gently, sharing retorts.

The wind, it teases; branches sway,
While critters plan a wild ballet.
A rabbit in a tiny tie,
Sips lemonade as passing flies.

So come and join this merry spree,
Where laughter bounces like a bee!
In frolic, breeze, and nature's cheer,
The woodland's joy is ever near.

Chronicles of the Barky Guardians

In leafy gowns, the guardians stand,
With barky shields, to make a band.
They chuckle deep, while crows debate,
On who should carry home the weight.

A chipmunk dons a crown out wide,
Barking orders, full of pride.
He tries to lead, but stumbles 'round,
While laughter echoes through the ground.

The owls follow with a hoot and flap,
In search of snacks, perhaps a map.
With breadcrumbs trailing, they all munch,
On curious recipes for lunch.

So join the jest and face the trees,
Where guardians dance with boundless glee.
In barky tales of silly deeds,
Nature thrives on laughter's seeds.

Whispered Quests of the Cloven Tracks

A goat in boots, oh what a sight,
He scales the hill with all his might.
He trips and rolls, yet with a grin,
Declares, 'This battle I will win!'

In trails of mud, the otters slide,
While raccoons vow to join the ride.
They scheme for snacks beneath the moon,
Inventing dishes, quite a tune!

In whispered quests, they share their fares,
With jokes exchanged like summer airs.
A deer with specs checks each direction,
Finding treasure with pure perfection.

So laughter leads their merry way,
In grassy fields where shadows play.
On cloven tracks, friendships abound,
In joyful moments all around.

The Serpent's Trail in the Golden Leaves

A serpent slithers with a style,
Twisting through leaves, it stops a while.
With winks and nods to passing friends,
He jokes that nothing ever ends.

The leaves are crunchy, what a treat,
The serpent rolls to dance his beat.
While chipmunks sneeze with nutty glee,
They wrap him up in leaves like tea.

A party forms with twirls and sprays,
As nature giggles through its plays.
The breeze joins in with tickles bright,
A festival of pure delight!

So if you wander 'neath the trees,
And hear the laughter on the breeze,
Just know the serpent leads the way,
To fun, to joy, a sunny day.

The Lure of the Lost Path

There's a path that goes nowhere, so they say,
A shoehorn for ankles that wish to play.
Take a step, then two, maybe try for a third,
You'd think that the trees are just waiting for a word.

But the squirrels all giggle as they dart and they dash,
While the hedgehogs are rolling in a fashionable flash.
The moss says, "Why hurry? Come lounge on my mat!"
As the crickets debate which is better, a hat.

Mud puddles beckon with a gleeful delight,
Jump in! Splash the toads! Oh, what a sight!
The path twists and tangles like spaghetti on a hook,
If you're not careful, you'll end up in a book.

So if you seek adventure, just follow the cheer,
But mind where you wander, a bear might be near!
With a chuckle and roar, he may join in your feasts,
Uninvited, of course, but he's a joy, at least!

Dances in the Dappled Light

In the sunbeams that wiggle, the fairies are bold,
They tango with shadows, they jive, and they fold.
With dainty little steps, oh, how they flit!
Beware of that mushroom – it's no place to sit!

A breeze tickles leaves, they shimmy and sway,
Is that a fox tootling a tune on a tray?
And if you see rabbits with top hats galore,
They might just be planning a dance-off in store!

The grass, it rolls over, a carpet of green,
While woodpeckers drum to the nature scene.
With the sun as their spotlight, they dance with flair,
But don't step on a snail! That's a comedic scare!

When twilight arrives, the disco ball glows,
The critters all gather, in awe of their shows.
With giggles and grumbles, they whirl through the night,
A wildwood cabaret, oh, what a delight!

Threads of Nature's Serenade

In the tapestry woven with nature's own thread,
The flowers are gossiping, each one in its bed.
While daisies are blushing, the roses just pout,
"Tell us a secret, or we'll start to shout!"

A bumblebee buzzes, a joker of sorts,
He chirps in good humor while dodging his shorts.
The dandelions puff, they're tickled and spry,
As they float in the air - oh my, oh my!

Spider webs glisten, they sparkle in jest,
Signaling spiders, the dance partners best.
If you hear a cackle, it's a bird with a quirk,
Belly-laughing loudly, oh, what a perk!

So listen closely, dear friend, to the sounds all around,
Nature's orchestra plays, sweet and profound.
With chuckles and chirps, the world's filled with cheer,
A symphony of laughter, that's perfectly clear!

The Language of Leaves

The leaves are all whispering, secrets they share,
With rustles and giggles filling the air.
"Did you hear about Acorn?" the Maple does tease,
"Last I saw him, he was lost in the breeze!"

With a flick and a flutter, they gossip and jive,
About raccoons in masks who think they can drive.
The Oak shakes his limbs, "I'm wise, don't you know?
But watch out for squirrels, they've got quite the show!"

"Who needs a therapist? We've got the whole wood,
With laughter and twirls that lift spirits for good.
We dare you to dance with the wind at your back,
It's a wacky parade down the leaf-laden track!"

As twilight descends, the voices grow low,
But the chuckles keep rising, they're stealing the show.
So next time you venture on paths that you roam,
Just stop, hear the whispers, and feel right at home!

Dance of the Fireflies

In the glade where the night lights play,
Tiny sparks make a grand ballet.
They flicker and twirl in the dark sky bright,
Blinking like stars that forgot it's night.

A bug in a top hat begins to prance,
With a ladybug waiting to take a chance.
The moon giggles from her lofty throne,
As fireflies dance in a spotlight of their own.

Crickets chirp their offbeat tune,
While frogs clap along, quite out of their tune.
Each flash a jest, a rippling tease,
In this nightly show, they aim to please.

So gather round, don't miss the show,
When the fireflies put on their glow!
With laughter and light, the forest is alive,
In this haphazard dance, we all shall thrive.

Enigma of the Forest's Heartbeat

In the depths where sunlight fades,
A rustling sound beneath the glades.
Is it a secret, a riddle so slick?
Or just a squirrel playing a trick?

The trees gossip in whispers low,
Admitting they've seen a raccoon show.
But why the owl with its exaggerated eye,
Is it puzzled, or just a little sly?

Mushrooms giggle, they can't keep still,
As shadows dance just over the hill.
The porcupine says, "I know what's true!"
But can't remember just what it knew.

Every snap of a twig, every rustle near,
Is just the forest having a cheer.
So let's embrace this comical spree,
In the heartbeat of mystery and glee.

Cadence of the Rustling Grass

In fields where the grass begins to sway,
The wind plays tunes, oh what a display!
Each blade a dancer, tall and spry,
They shimmy and shake as the breezes fly.

A worm joins in, with moves quite absurd,
Wiggling along, without a word.
Grasshoppers leap to a rhythm so fine,
Creating a melody, one of a kind.

But wait, what's that? A clumsy mouse,
Trying to groove but losing its house.
With a twist and a tumble, it joins the show,
In the jive of the grass, all's aglow!

So sway with the rhythm, let laughter pass,
Join the parade of the rustling grass.
In nature's concert, everyone's a star,
Even the shy, kinda weird ones, bizarre!

The Solace of Twilight Shadows

As dusk settles soft with a gentle yawn,
Shadows stretch far, embracing the dawn.
A bat flutters by, playing peek-a-boo,
Daring the deer to see what it'll do.

Crickets tune in, each voice a delight,
Singing their hearts out to welcome the night.
The trees lean in, whisper secrets for free,
While the firewood chuckles, amusingly.

A shadow of something oddly wobbly,
Turns out to be just a lopsided jelly.
As frogs hop along with a splashy cheer,
In this twilight glow, there's nothing to fear.

So dance through the dusk, let your worries fall,
In the embrace of shadows, come one, come all.
Let laughter echo through branches so grand,
In the serene solitude, let joy take a stand.

The Serenade of Curling Vines

Beneath the boughs, the vines conspire,
With giggles soft, they dream and tire.
A ladybug rides on a sneezy leaf,
As clumsy ants dance, beyond belief.

The sunbeams drip like sweetened goo,
While turtles play hide and seek in dew.
A squirrel in shades, with a funky hat,
Turns cartwheels, squeaking 'Look at that!'

The flowers bloom with a wink so sly,
While butterflies giggle and flutter by.
Grasshoppers leap in a jovial trance,
While crickets hum a joyous dance.

Amidst the laughter, time takes a break,
As trees swap tales of a ten-foot snake.
In this funny realm, all creatures thrive,
Where nonsense rules, and joy's alive!

Rhapsody of the Hidden Glens

In hidden glens where gnomes do prance,
They juggle mushrooms in a silly dance.
A rabbit in glasses reads a sign,
That claims, 'Carrots are best served with wine!'

The brook giggles as it flows so clear,
With fish that sport party hats they wear.
A wise old owl hoots a riddle so sly,
'What's orange and juicy and loves to fly?'

With cobwebs spun like threads of lace,
Spiders scheme in their crafty space.
They launch a party, invite the bees,
But bumblebees are all too sneezy, please!

Fetch the confetti from the tall pine,
And let's toast to frogs dressed up in swine.
In these delightful, secret clearings,
The laughter echoes, at all the cheerings.

Ghosts of the Timbered Realm

Beneath the pines, ghostly shadows sway,
Whispering secrets of yesterday.
A cheeky specter plays peek-a-boo,
With a hollow laugh and a friendly boo!

The will-o'-the-wisps wear dazzling gowns,
And drift through the night with giggles and frowns.
They tickle the trees till they almost sway,
Chasing each other till the break of day.

Up in the treetops, two owls debate,
Who hoots the best, what's the best bait?
A ghostly fox joins with a sly grin,
'Let's scare the hikers, let the fun begin!'

With fireflies lighting a caper so bright,
Timber ghosts dance through the cool of night.
In laughter they weave their spectral glee,
In the realm of timber, wild and free.

Embracing the Heart of Thorns

In a thorny patch where mischief lies,
A hedgehog pricks just to catch a prize.
He juggles fruits with his tiny paws,
While giggling wildly at his own claws.

A rose with thorns tells tales of woe,
Yet cracks a smile with a radiant glow.
A bee stings lightly, butterfly screams,
'This thicket's a circus of silly dreams!'

A dandelion whispers, 'You should see,
The way the cacti play hide and seek!'
With giggles and snickers they tumble and roll,
While clumsy critters lose track of their goal.

In this sanctuary of laughs galore,
The thorns are guards but creatures adore.
Wild and whimsical, they frolic and sway,
In the heart of thorns, having the best day!

Reflections in the Mossy Glens

In the glens where the moss grows thick,
A squirrel once danced, oh what a trick!
He wiggled his tail, he frowned, he spun,
Chased by a crow who thought it was fun.

The brook giggled, splashing in the sun,
While frogs croaked jokes, oh how they run!
A deer in the shade peered out with a grin,
Wondering how squirrels could dance on a whim.

A rabbit nearby laughed, 'It's all in the moves!'
'But careful,' he said, 'of squirrels who grooved!'
For in every twist and every silly taunt,
Lies a lesson learned from the woodlands' jaunt.

When the sun sets low, the glens softly sigh,
As creatures whisper their quick alibi.
'Twas a day full of laughter, a day full of glee,
In the reflections of woods, where all can be free.

Murmuring Brook Beneath the Stars

Under stars that twinkle with quirky delight,
The brook shared tales on this enchanting night.
'The fish here are wise, or so I've been told,
They wear little hats and think they are bold.'

An owl hooted softly, 'I've heard of their fame,
Dressed in bright colors, they play silly games!'
While nearby a raccoon, snacking on pie,
Said, 'I'm starting a band, you can even try!'

The crickets all chirped, tapping their feet,
To the tunes of the brook, they found quite the beat.
And the stars overhead seemed to giggle and sway,
As they listened to fish sporting hats made of clay.

So if you wander where laughter meets night,
Join in the fun, it's an absolute fright!
For under the cosmos, where shadows may creep,
Is a gathering of chirps, where dreams never sleep.

Echoes in the Hollowed Trunks

In trees with great hollows, secrets abound,
Echoes of laughter float softly around.
A woodpecker knocked a rhythm so grand,
While a beetle claimed he had a rock band.

Behind the bark lived a gnome full of cheer,
He painted his fungi with frolicking sneers.
'Come dance with me, friend, on this stump by the brook,
We'll celebrate nature, come take a good look!'

The fox rolled her eyes, 'You gnomes are all nuts,
But join us for chips, just no more silly cuts!'
Yet despite all the grumbling, the laughter still thrived,
For in hollowed-out trunks, the kernels derived.

So when you meander and hear echoes near,
Remember the joy that draws friends so near.
In the heart of the woods, though it can be absurd,
The tales of these trunks are forever unheard.

Twilight Tales of the Forest Floor

As twilight sneaks in, tales simmer and swirl,
With mushrooms at tea, and foxes that twirl.
A badger recited his favorite myth,
Of a hat-wearing owl who danced with a slith.

The fireflies wiggled to the beats of the night,
While raccoons brought snacks, oh what a sight!
'The cheese was from dreams of the truffle variety,
Now join in the fun, taste the wild hilarity!'

Under darkened skies, the laughter took flight,
With beetles in bow ties all ready to bite.
And the trees, like old friends, echoed their glee,
In tales of the forest, forever carefree.

So gather, dear friends, on this floor of delight,
In the twilight's embrace, 'neath the moon's soft light.
For there in the whispers, amid giggles so pure,
Are stories unwritten, of joy that endures.

The Unfolding of Nature's Secrets

Leaves rustle, secrets shared,
Squirrels dance, all unprepared.
Mushrooms laugh with cheeky glee,
Beneath the shade of an old tree.

Frogs croak jokes, a nightly show,
While owls hoot with laughter so.
The brook babbles, spilling tales,
Of dragonflies on tiny sails.

Beneath the stars, the critters play,
Chasing fireflies that feel gay.
Every rustle, every noise,
Echoes the heart of forest joys.

The Joy of Verdant Rebirth

Spring arrives with quirks and quirks,
Trees wear bloom like silly shirts.
Blossoms giggle, colors bright,
Dancing in the morning light.

Bunnies hop with playful grace,
Chasing flowers in a race.
Ladybugs in polka dots,
Join the party, tying knots.

The sun winks from up high,
While robins whistle, oh so sly.
Ants march in their tiny bands,
All sharing snacks from picnic lands.

Secrets of the Forest's Embrace

Whispers float where shadows creep,
Furry creatures start to leap.
From behind a bush, a glance,
And hedgehogs join the dance.

The pines tell tales in twisting vines,
While raccoons scheme in straight lines.
With every rustle, giggies flow,
Forest mischief starts to grow.

Toadstools play a game of hide,
As chipmunks burst with cheerful pride.
Under stars, they share their cheer,
With silly stories, without fear.

The Whisper of Dusk's Caress

As twilight paints the sky with gold,
Fireflies gather, brave and bold.
Crickets strum their soothing tunes,
While raccoons sneak and share their spoons.

The moon peeks out, a cheeky grin,
As nighttime antics start to spin.
Owls swoop down to tease the night,
And shadows dodge with pure delight.

In the hush, laughter swells,
Nature's secrets, silly spells.
Dusk unveils its playful charm,
Wrapping the woods in a warm arm.

Murmurs Beneath the Ancient Boughs

Under the leaves, a squirrel chatters,
Telling tales of acorns and nuts that splatters.
A deer with glasses reads a map,
Getting lost in a ferny nap.

The owls hoot jokes with great delight,
While crickets dance to the moon's soft light.
A raccoon steals snacks with a grin,
While the hedgehogs giggle, letting him in.

Bees in bow ties buzzing with flair,
Trading sweet secrets without a care.
A fox in a cloak acts oh-so-fine,
As the chipmunks argue over who'll dine.

Laying on mushrooms like fluffy beds,
The woodland chucklers nod their heads.
Beneath the boughs, laughter flows free,
In a riot of joy, just wait and see.

Lullabies of the Verdant Shadows

Beneath the shade, where the ferns twirl,
A tortoise in shades starts to whirl.
The rabbits hold court, telling tall tales,
While the snails race with their slow-paced trails.

A bear strums a lute, singing off-key,
And the tribes of birds dance with glee.
Fireflies laugh in a shimmering line,
Glowing like stars, oh-so-fine.

The trees sway gently, their branches nod,
As the frogs leap in a silly squad.
A turtle tells jokes of ancient lore,
While the salmon bellyflop to roar.

In dappled light, the giggles resound,
Where mischief and fun abound.
Under the green, it's a joyful spree,
Singing lullabies with pure glee.

Whispers of the Woodland Spirits

In the thicket, the sprites plot and plan,
Offering advice to a bemused man.
With tricks up their sleeves, they play and tease,
Turning his shoelaces into a tease.

With leaves as their hats and sticks for wands,
They race through the trees like playful fronds.
The mushrooms giggle as they tease the fawns,
As frogs don crowns made of dawn's soft yawns.

A wise old owl gives puns from his perch,
While the wise trees guffaw, giving a lurch.
A raccoon in a tux makes quite a fuss,
As he claims the squirrels are stealing his dust!

From roots to crowns, merriment swells,
A symphony of laughter that truly compels.
With each playful wind, a secret's in thrall,
Forest frolics enchant one and all.

Songs from the Heart of the Forest

In a grove where the chuckles never cease,
A bear plays games, seeking no peace.
The hedgehogs hoot while spinning about,
While the woodpeckers drum with a shout.

The balsam trees sway and sing along,
With a tone that is merry, a sweet, subtle song.
The raccoon hosts parties and serves up a pie,
While the rabbits toast marshmallows up high.

The dappled sun shines, the shadows jiggle,
As chipmunks join in with a silly giggle.
A fox tells tales of mischief and glee,
As all woodland creatures dance round the tree.

From dawn to dusk, the joy is alive,
With secrets of laughter that help us thrive.
Through the heart of the woods, beneath the day's light,
Songs echo with cheer, from morning till night.

Rhythms of the Twilight Grove

In the grove where shadows dance,
Squirrels prance in a nutty trance.
Rabbits giggle, chasing their tails,
Echoing laughter floats in the trails.

Crickets strum their tiny strings,
While owls sport their silver rings.
A raccoon juggles with pine cones,
As whispers tease in silly tones.

Fireflies blink their little lights,
Creating sparks on starry nights.
Frogs croak tunes offbeat and bold,
Sharing secrets none have told.

And when the moon begins to glow,
The trees start winking, don't you know?
A party in the wildwood deep,
Where even dreams take silly leaps.

The Soft Footfall of the Nightingale

A nightingale with a clumsy step,
Sings off-key, but gives it a rep.
Its friends all chuckle, what a delight,
To frolic under the moonlight bright.

In the branches, the fireflies bicker,
While raccoons play tag, oh, a snicker!
Tails all tangled in branches and leaves,
Dark night filled with such bubbly eaves.

The night whispers jokes of silly fame,
As hedgehogs roast marshmallows aflame.
They laugh and snort at the tales they spin,
While watching the moon dip down with a grin.

When dawn approaches, with a yawn and a blink,
The woodland revelers take time to think.
"Let's meet again!" the chorus declares,
In the light of day, their antics like fares.

Tales Spun by the Wandering Wind

The wind carries whispers and fits of glee,
Telling tales of the squirrel and spree.
A dance through the branches, a twist and a turn,
Leaves flutter down, for giggles they learn.

A beaver taps out a playful beat,
While porcupines shuffle on little feet.
With laughter like ripples, they giggle and sway,
Chasing sunsets into a colorful fray.

The wind tells of goats who play hopscotch,
Leaping from rocks, no need for a watch.
They stumble and tumble with joyous shouts,
As nature joins in with funny bouts.

Then owls wink knowingly from the trees,
As chipmunks giggle in the gentle breeze.
Every twist of the wind brings a smile so sly,
In this world where giggles venture high.

Whirl of the Maple Leaves

Maple leaves swirl in a colorful flow,
Dancing around like a good circus show.
With each gust of laughter, they twirl with style,
Creating a whirlwind of joy all the while.

A bunny hops in the middle with flair,
Trying to dodge what's up in the air.
The leaves laugh and shout, "Catch us if you can!"
As the squirrel scoffs, "I'm the speedy man!"

A chorus of crows joins the raucous play,
Squawking and cawing, in wild disarray.
The wind whips through, tickling their wings,
Adding a rhythm fit for clownish kings.

As evening falls and the fun starts to fade,
The leaves whisper secrets of the pranks they played.
With a final whirl, they settle down slow,
Dreaming of tomorrows, where silliness grows.

Nature's Ink on Bark

The tree trunks scribble tales,
Of squirrels stealing acorns,
While ants march in parade,
To toast to their great fortune.

A woodpecker drums a beat,
On a log that's quite off-key,
The mushrooms dance in circles,
With moves that you can't unsee.

Rabbits gossip as they hop,
About the fox with bad fur,
Who tried to impress the doe,
But fell into a stir.

The sun sets with a laugh,
As shadows leap and prance,
Nature's script forever flows,
In this lively, leafy dance.

Tender Footfalls in the Underbrush

Each step a crunch beneath,
Leaves gossip of your ways,
The crabgrass throws a party,
For those who dare to play.

A mole peeks from his burrow,
Wonders what's that racket?
A human tripping over roots,
With snacks stuck in their jacket.

Bunnies peek from tangled grass,
Snickering at the sight,
Of a clumsy explorer,
Who thinks he's quite the fright.

With every funny stumble,
Nature claps and grins,
Life here is a comedy,
Where laughter always wins.

Whims of the Elusive Faerie Trails

They flit with giggles bright,
In petals made of dreams,
But leave behind a riddle,
To puzzle all the teams.

A leaf might turn to gold,
If you dance with just the right tune,
Yet trip over a flower pot,
And they vanish just like noon.

Their laughter drips like honey,
From branches near and far,
While fireflies take bets,
On how swift you are.

But catch them in your net,
And they'll tickle you with glee,
For the faeries love a chuckle,
As they twirl around a tree.

Starlit Conversations in the Pines

The pines lean in to hear,
What crickets have to say,
As stars blink in a rhythm,
To guide the night's ballet.

With every rustle softly,
A tale slips through the leaves,
Of owls who wear spectacles,
And the webs that spiders weave.

A campfire crackles loudly,
With stories grand and bold,
Of raccoons who steal sandwiches,
More brazen than the old.

The night air hums with laughter,
And secrets shared through sighs,
In the glow of twinkling lights,
Under vast, enchanting skies.

The Dance of the Dappled Sunlight

In the forest, squirrels prance,
Chasing shadows, taking a chance.
Leaves do giggle, branches sway,
As the sunlight joins the play.

Bunnies hop in silly lines,
Underneath the twisting vines.
Frolicking through hidden glades,
Planning grand, ridiculous parades.

The dappled light does tap its feet,
To a rhythm oh-so-sweet.
Nature claps with glee and cheer,
As the joyous critters appear.

In this caper, magic's spun,
Every leaf's a little pun.
Laughter echoes, wild and free,
In this leafy jubilee.

Resonance of Crow's Call

A crow croaks out his best joke,
While all the deer, they just choke.
His caws echo through the trees,
Tickling branches, stirring leaves.

The rabbits gather, ears all perked,
Wondering why their funny quirks.
The crow winks, quite the charmer,
His punchlines causing quite the drama!

A squirrel giggles, rolling about,
Witty banter without a doubt.
With a flap, the crow takes flight,
Making mischief, what a sight!

As the sun sets, they share a cheer,
For jesters thrive when friends are near.
In this realm of giggly brawl,
Nature's laughter, the best of all.

Spirit of the Boundless Canopy

Underneath the leafy dome,
Creatures frolic, far from home.
A raccoon with a hat so grand,
Turns the forest into a band.

The owls hoot their wise advice,
Mixing secrets with a slice.
The raccoon jigs, all in black,
While trees sway, letting humor crack.

Foxes whisper, tales of loot,
Inventing legends, oh so cute.
In this canopy, joy takes flight,
With critters dancing through the night.

Every rustle, every sound,
Brings laughter to this leafy ground.
The spirit here, so light and free,
In this mirthful jubilee.

Enchanted Paths of the Moonlit Glade

In the glade where shadows play,
Moonbeams lead a funny ballet.
Frogs in tuxedos leap and croak,
While owls wink and have a poke.

The mushrooms grin, quite the sights,
Cheering on the whimsical flights.
Baboons bumble in puffy shoes,
On enchanted paths, they can't lose.

Each flicker brings contagious glee,
As fireflies dance with jubilee.
In this realm of night's embrace,
Laughter echoes in every space.

So follow the trails of light and cheer,
Every twist will bring you near.
To a world where chuckles reign,
In the moonlit glade, joy is plain.

Echoes in the Untamed Grove

A fox in boots on a tree stump sits,
With a monocle and tales of funny bits.
He chats with a squirrel, a wise old chap,
Who's plotting a flight in a big acorn cap.

The owls chuckle low, as night creeps near,
"Who's there?" asks one, "Oh dear, oh dear!"
The raccoons dance round in a wobbly groove,
Serving nuts with a side of their best movie move.

Beneath the branches where shadows play,
A rabbit's convinced it's opposite day.
He hops to the left, then back to the right,
While cracking jokes under the silver moonlight.

In a trunk so wide, there's a party theme,
With barky confetti and a bubbling stream.
The critters all gather, their spirits aglow,
Echoes of laughter where the wild breezes blow.

Secrets of the Ancient Canopy

Up high where the giants stretch towards the sky,
A parrot named Polly is learning to fly.
With a feathered cap and a snazzy tie,
She jokes with the bluejays who chuckle and sigh.

The wise old tortoise, so slow and so grand,
Tells stories of shenanigans, never planned.
With every deep breath, he crafts a tall tale,
Of how he once raced a snail down a trail.

A deer with a crown made of daisies spins,
Inviting the critters to join in her wins.
They prance and they twirl, such a sight to behold,
As laughter erupts, two squirrels grow bold.

In shadows and sunlight, they play hide and seek,
While a fox plays the flute, so smooth, not meek.
Secrets abound in this whimsical land,
Where fun is the law and laughter is planned.

Murmurs Beneath the Leafy Veil

Under the cover where sunlight is shy,
A raccoon reads poetry, oh my, oh my!
With a tail like a feather, all fluffy and grand,
He quotes every line while the owls clap their hands.

A hedgehog with glasses writes poems so bold,
Of lost socks and biscuits and stories retold.
He scribbles and giggles, a real charming sight,
As the crickets all hum through the soft night.

In the whispers of branches, the laughter flows free,
A gathering chorus of joy, oh me!
The beavers build boats just to float in a stream,
While the frogs croak their tunes, living the dream.

With critters so clever and spirits so bright,
They weave all their tales with twinkle and light.
Beneath leafy canopies where humor prevails,
The forest dances with magical trails.

Tales of the Forgotten Glade

In dappled sunlight, where odd things roam,
A turtle recites verses as if they were home.
His audience, chuckling, is all out of breath,
As a chipmunk tells stories of snack time and theft.

With mushrooms for tables and acorns for chairs,
The critters convene, spinning tales of their snares.
A goat in a jacket brings snacks on a plate,
While the fireflies dance in a neon debate.

An old wooden stump holds secrets galore,
From wacky adventures to lore evermore.
They gather around, sharing laughter and cheer,
As the night wraps them snugly, with joy oh so near.

In this glade full of giggles where stories entwine,
Where every nutty mishap is humor divine.
They forge bonds of friendship with each funny tale,
Together in mischief, they happily sail.

www.ingramcontent.com/pod-product-compliance
Lightning Source LLC
Chambersburg PA
CBHW071854160426
43209CB00003B/544